Stronger Than the Current

Mark Thalman

A Publication of The Poetry Box®

Poems ©2021 Mark Thalman
All rights reserved.

Editing, Book & Cover Design: Shawn Aveningo Sanders
Cover Painting: Mark Thalman
Author photo: Carole Thalman

No part of this book may be reproduced in any manner whatsoever without permission from the author, except in the case of brief quotations embodied in critical essays, reviews and articles.

ISBN: 978-1-948461-75-7
Printed in the United States of America.
Wholesale Distribution via Ingram.

Published by The Poetry Box®, 2021
Portland, Oregon
ThePoetryBox.com

For Carole

Contents

Some History
Logging the Umpqua, the Tree Topper   9
The Spar Tree, the High Climber   10
Marcola Ridge   11
Salmonberry Mountain, 1911   12
Logging Camp, 1921   13
Tillamook Burn, 1933   14
Cone Picking   15
Widow-Makers   16
Hanging Up the Spurs, the Tree Topper   17

The Daily Forecast
Elegy for a Common Field   21
Arlington, Oregon, 1956   22
Celilo Falls   23
Eastern Oregon   25
Finley's Pasture   26
Late July: Harvest   27
David Hill Road   28
Wilson River: First Outing after Quadruple Bypass   29
Hiking the Wilson River Trail   30
Ten Feet of Rain   31
Rain Country   32
Extended Forecast: More Rain   33
March Weather   34
Escape   35
Dawson Pond   36
Thatcher Road   37

The Daily Forecast	38
Columbus Day Storm	39
Mapleton	41
Neskowin	42
Nehalem	43
Rockfishing	44
Winter Storm	46
Acknowledgments	47
Praise for *Stronger Than the Current*	49
About the Author	51
About The Poetry Box®	52

Some History

*They say the first spar is the tallest,
but that's all hokum; everyone you climb
is the tallest.*

—Ken Kesey

Logging the Umpqua, the Tree Topper

I sink spurs into bark, pull the rope secure.
The wind makes long vowel sounds
trying to speak
one word.

Down the mountain,
two field hawks
patient as gods
glide across a meadow
to the far ridge.

I use my axe, then saw
until the top leans,
bending the tree
like a stem of ripe wheat.

When you hear the wood begin to crack, splinter,
hold tight—that fir comes springing back.
I ride the whipping sway.

Below, branches snap. The crown explodes:
hundreds of years old, the moan.

The Spar Tree, the High Climber

After topping the crown
and the fir stops waving about,
I slip out of my ropes
to stand on top of this flagpole,
doing a little soft-shoe,
flapping arms, yahooing
high in the wind.

To descend, I kneel awkward as a child
trying to crawl off a tall chair,
snap the bindings secure,
then throw my metal helmet
so it skips through air
like a stone across water.

I am a mountain climber
rappelling a sheer cliff,
swing out into space,
pendulum back, or a spider
elevatoring down a thread.

My boots strike earth
moments before my yellow hat.

Marcola Ridge

In a small clearing, while cruising timber,
I discover these logs no wider than telephone poles—
all laid out: spaced regular and half buried
like the ribs of something prehistoric.

They had been here, the spotted oxen,
snorting steam in the cool morning,
a dozen in a team: bulls
straining against their yokes,
the chain, the dragging weight of logs
heavy as a laden boxcar—

like one of those blocks
when the Egyptians built pyramids,
that chunk slides slowly over the skids.

Usually, a timber will decay so bad,
I can break it easy as a loaf of bread,
but this wood worn smooth has been preserved.
Boys swabbed on whale oil to help the loads slip.

And cussing as though a hoof had crushed his foot,
the puncher must have walloped oxen flanks,
condemning each beast
to some terrible eternity.

I stay a while longer, remembering Grandfather,
who told me how he worked on such a crew,
before his memory faded
like this road the forest reclaims,
then go about my business of counting trees.

Salmonberry Mountain, 1911

Working with double-bitted axes
sharp enough to get a good shave,
fallers hew out slots
to fit springboards into bark.

Balancing on these planks, chips fly
like ants gnawing a giant stalk.

After the wedged out cut, big enough
for a lumberjack to lay down
and pretend he might be crushed,
they rip with a crosscut saw
the entire afternoon,
until the tree begins to snap.

Leaping like bucks,
each man searches for safety—
playing the odds
the fir will not fall crazy,
pounding them with one blow
as a sledge drives a stake.

A tremendous cracking fractures air,
the immense weight roaring through space . . .
slamming the ground—
exploding limbs, shrapnel.

Where the crown used to be
is a hole in the canopy
like looking up
from the bottom of a grave.

Logging Camp, 1921

Dad rigs spar lines,
while Mom stirs stew
on a wood burning stove.
She tries growing tomatoes
where sun cleaves through the forest,
but has better luck
bringing down ducks
along the river.

I go to school in a make-shift boxcar.
I've had the same teacher for seven years,
Mrs. Brunig: silver hair, bad teeth, Medusa stare.
Her voice, heavy as a baseball bat, stops any mischief.

The bunkhouse crew leaves early.
Most days everyone comes back.
If they are carrying a body on a stretcher,
don't ask. As returning from battle,
hardhats like WW-I helmets,
their downcast eyes
tell the story.

Tillamook Burn, 1933

Jagged as a king's crown,
with a diameter of nearly six feet,
the rings of this stump are impossible to count.

A decayed tooth, the middle is hollowed out.
Weathered gray as granite, the thick shell
has become its own monument.

A dark blaze stretching down one side
testifies to where flames
seared through bark.

Relic of a fire so hot,
ash like snow piled a foot deep,
fell on ships hundreds of miles out to sea.

Violent winds created by heat
powerful as a hydrogen bomb
uprooted giant firs, vaporized streams.

All caused by a logging cable
scraping over bark
igniting a spark into tinder.

Cone Picking

I walk up the thick bark of this fir
anchoring my feet with spurs, hands
pulling in slack rope.

At the limbs, I free climb
like a mountaineer,
stand on a thin branch,
a tentative ledge.

The wind up here
can make the best climber dizzy.
Wing walking, I tether myself
to the trunk,

gather a gunnysack full
and drop it over the side:

a whole forest
falling through air.

Widow-Makers

High in a fir, a dead limb—
On the next breath of wind,

call it chance
this branch breaks . . .

If one of the logging crew gets clubbed,
it's only fifty-fifty they get up.

A hard hat can't ward off
heavy artillery.

If the top of a tree leans like a drunk,
I'm not too proud to circle around.

The hammer is cocked.
Fate pulls the trigger.

Hanging Up the Spurs, the Tree Topper

A strong gust of wind sets this fir swaying.
Through high swells, I lose my grip. The rope slips,
and the tree, a fist, slams me in the stomach.

Unable to catch my breath, a red-light flashes on
in my head. The only way I know to make a living
is to climb these giant's—no net.

Having more close calls than I care to admit,
it's time to quit, pass the spurs to the burly kid,
who lettered in wrestling and can get a strong hold.

Already, bruises, black roses, are blooming
on my arms and chest. In my knapsack
is a bottle of liniment.

Tonight, I can tell my wife,
she no longer has to worry
if the phone rings before I get home.

The Daily Forecast

Elegy for a Common Field

Gone are the deer trails and coyote tracks,
the century-old firs, the giant oak
with the tree fort.

Gone is the snag the kestrel used for a perch,
moles forming miniature mountain ranges,
spiders spinning webs
across newly plowed furrows,
so threads resembled thousands of wires
stretching across America.

Gone is the topsoil
dumped in the ravine, the wheat
that flourished every summer,
the slant of evening light
turning grain the shade of champagne.

Gone are the goats
that occasionally wandered over
from Jones's farm, the milk cow
who enjoyed walkabouts,
red-tailed hawks appearing
after the combines harvested
to eat eviscerated mice.

All because a father dies, and his grown children
inherit the land, money changes hands,
a developer threatens to sue
to get an urban boundary moved,
and a city council votes
unanimously for their idea of progress.

Arlington, Oregon, 1956

The railroad and highway snaked along the river.
Up the slope, huge oaks shaded yards
on blistering summer afternoons.

In the evening, sun dropping below
the crest of the gorge, the entire town
would fall into shadow, while the far side
of the Columbia still baked.

Mom said, "This is the last time
we will see this place . . .
When the dam is finished
everything will be under water
like the castle in your fishbowl."

I had visions of salmon
swimming down streets,
and slipping through
empty windows.

Tugging her sleeve,
"Will they move the trees?"

"No," she said, and fell silent.

Celilo Falls

The frothing river cascades
over basalt cliffs, pounding
giant drums, thundering for miles.
Salmon launch themselves
out of white water—
fall back into the roaring torrent.

For ten thousand years,
men have come here
to spear Chinook
or stand on scale slick,
mist covered platforms
with long-handled dip nets.

When the flood gates closed,
the river began to rise,
and the spectacular rumbling
which had filled the air
for millions of years slowly died.
Families lining the rim
were consumed by silence.

While the water inched higher,
planks and poles from scaffolds
drifted away like their lives.
The next to drown were petroglyphs,
village sites, and burial grounds,
under a deep lake
to generate cheap electricity.

In the legend, five Swallow Sisters
built a barrier preventing the salmon
from returning. Coyote tricked them,
destroyed their dam, and the flood
washed away the land leaving Celilo Falls.
May Coyote bring back the falls again.

Eastern Oregon

Out here, miles from anywhere,
coyotes, cattle, and sun become your companions.

Hills roll and fold, a sea of giant swells,
then flatten out, lie calm, in bleaching summer heat.

When evening unveils its stars,
life shrinks under the universe.

For centuries, Nez Perce came to trade for Columbia salmon,
then Pioneers snaked wagons down the Blue Mountains.

Even today, dust devils coil up,
and rivers cut deep gorges.

Sage grows low so wind can go where it wants—
whistling through wire fences.

Finley's Pasture

Four Belgians, ebony titans, long retired,
graze the green hillside. Heads raised, ears erect,
they snort loudly, clearing their nostrils to decipher the wind.

Flexing legs into motion, their hooves pounding
with stronger and greater strides, the earth resonates.
They circle tighter and tighter until there is no escape.

Only six, she is barely able to reach their stomachs.
Nickering softly, they nudge her gently in the side,
sniffing what she hides.

Coat pockets bulging, she offers Gravensteins
gathered from her family's orchard,
which borders the horse's pasture.

Unable to reach these apples through the fence,
they lower their heads as if giving thanks. Soft muzzles
and rubbery lips brush her outstretched palms.

They crunch the shiny fruit to pulp and foaming mustaches.
With complete joy, yet calm, she pats their chests and legs.
As though she was one of their own, they nuzzle her.

Beginning to graze again, she stands with them,
a member of the herd. Primal instincts flowing back and forth,
a language all their own, only they can understand.

Late July: Harvest

Inside a small thicket, surrounded
by ripe wheat, a doe and fawn sleep.
Through afternoon heat, a combine,
a giant beast, rumbles steadily toward them . . .
The deer stay low, ears folded, eyes closed
against the whirlwind of noise, glinting steel.
Not until the sun and moon briefly share the sky,
do they rise and step cautiously
to the edge of the field, fading
in the dimming light,
the warm breeze pungent
with hay and fallen plums
from the abandoned orchard.

David Hill Road

Whoever owned this '54 Chevy sedan
must not have been a mechanic
or a conjurer who could raise machinery
from the dead. Instead, too cheap
to have it towed, the car rests
in a traffic of weeds.
Seed tufts poke through the grill
like steam issuing from an overheated radiator.
Plum trees blossoming form clouds of exhaust,
while a blackberry vine, a policeman, taps
at the driver's window.
On clear summer nights,
under the bright headlight of the moon,
crickets hum a well-tuned engine.
The Chevrolet appears to be speeding through
the soft blue landscape into tomorrow—
rushing into the future
of its own slow decay.

Wilson River: First Outing after Quadruple Bypass

Along the upper reaches, fog hangs thick
against basalt cliffs—steep mountain sides,
where wisps slide through fir tops.

Mist coalesces on pine needles—
drops reflecting sky,
shining as if they had their own light.

Walking this path with my wife,
we pass by bright green carpets
of moss and bracken.

All this color sloshed higher
than a full rack of antlers,
a flood of lichen.

Stopping at the meadow's edge,
we sight the tallest fir,
top dead—hit by lightning.

Bark still bears the scar
the bolt traveled, as does my chest
from the heart surgeon's scalpel.

Sometimes, eagles perch here—
survey the fast curving ribbon
running high from snow melt.

Having survived off the winterkill of elk,
it is nearly time for them to feast on spring run salmon,
add more sticks to the nest started last year.

Hiking the Wilson River Trail

A mossy log, pointing downhill, drips
minute drops stored from the last storm

while far below, the river runs clear,
flowing along a mosaic of boulders,

splashing against the side of an outcrop,
releasing foam and spray,

then smoothing out for a stretch
before rolling into rapids, frothing white . . .

The forest is a huge heart pumping back to the sea.
After bypass surgery, I could only take small steps.

Sun playing through the canopy,
my surgeon's voice comes back to me,

"Keep moving."

Ten Feet of Rain

Annual Rainfall in the Tillamook Forest

The rain glistens like salmon scales
on the tip of an eagle's beak, decorates
ends of pine needles with ornaments,
strips maples of their last gold leaves,
flakes tumbling in a stream.

The rain invades every valley,
dances like a madman across the roof all night,
falls hard and fast
as if someone is pouring
water from a glass.

The rain says its name,
and the chant blesses the forest.
Windshield wipers join the chorus,
while some curse the long cold days,
the dripping away of their existence.

Rain Country

To say it rains in the Tillamook Forest
is like saying the sun shines in the Sahara.

Sometimes locals go crazy
from the constant drip
only summer can shut off.

Winter days wash your psyche
until it is wrinkled as skin
that's been in a bath too long.

Some say living here is torture.
Others say they wouldn't have it
any other way.

Extended Forecast: More Rain

The rain raps at windows
with thousands of little fists,
fades to mist, ghosting the hills.

The rain sprays from the back of a coyote
giving himself a good shake, trickles
its way back to the sea . . .
a perpetual motion machine.

The rain makes circles mimicking trout
taking insects off the surface,
fills an abandoned coffee cup
spilling over like all the gray days of winter.

The rain is so pervasive
the Tillamook would stay
in their lodges and feast,
telling stories about the widow
who could not stop crying.

March Weather

Rapidly approaching
across forested hills
comes a crashing roar
I have never heard before.

I call my golden retriever and we run
trying to make it home
before the blast.

Reaching the front porch, hail—
twelve gauge shot
pelts the ground, ricochets off,
while the roof thunders
thousands of hammers.

I fix a cup of tea.
Sherlock laps his water urgently.
We listen to the storm begin to slacken—
the ticking of ice
like someone throwing rice,
a wedding of winter and spring.

Escape

Sunflowers
making
a break
for it
have gone
over
the garden
fence!

Each summer,
they nod
their heads
dropping
a few
more seeds.

Eventually,
they will
reach
the open
field.

Dawson Pond

The blue heron
blends in
to the curtain
of marsh grass
behind him.

Stalking the pond's edge,
he gorges himself
on small succulent frogs.

Minnows find his legs,
two reeds, a good place
to hide and rest
in the cloud shadow
hovering above them,
and like summer lightning
his beak strikes.

Thatcher Road

Half way to the next bend,
two deer cross the road,
but seeing me, freeze
on the center line
becoming statues.

On this section, cars barrel down—
bullet after bullet.

Walking toward them,
I wave my arms like tall antlers,
and they move on—
shadows merging into shadows,

leaving the road vacant
for crazed drivers
ripping through life.

The Daily Forecast

Early mornings, after the fog has risen,
I watch for wild goats
from my kitchen window.

If they meander
along the high ridges,
the day will be clear and sunny.

When the herd comes down
to graze in the meadow,
count on rain.

Spotting them somewhere in between,
I make my best guess, depending on which way
they happen to be going.

However, if they hide in the woods,
a big storm, a heavy fist,
is about to hit.

To predict the weather, I don't need
a barometer, radar, or satellite dish.
The goats are seldom wrong.

Columbus Day Storm

October 12, 1962

The western horizon is one huge ominous mass
rapidly growing darker. Barometric pressure
falling low, feels as though I am in a room
which doesn't have enough air.
Robins and sparrows have stopped singing...
Even the silence seems empty.

A stiff autumn breeze grows
becoming a continual stream, a river, then a stampede
smashing and pounding everything. In the side yard,
birch trees whip back and forth doing crazy calisthenics.
Windows bow and rattle. Wall switches glow yellow.
Under the couch, our orange cat huddles, shaking.

We camp in the hall, away from windows,
bedroom doors shut. The radio reports gusts
up to 179 mph clocked at Cape Blanco.
A heavy weight presses the sides of our house—
Outer walls rumble—
one long continuous freight.

By morning, the storm recedes.
So many trees are down, Eugene is a giant log jam.
Our shingles like birds have flown away.
My backboard and hoop lies fractured in the street.
Its wooden pole, thick as a man's leg, anchored in concrete
snapped off at the base.

We roast hot dogs in the fireplace.
On Dad's transistor: 48 dead, hundreds injured,
50,000 buildings damaged, millions in the dark,
15 billion board feet of timber blown down
from the coast all the way to Montana.
Enough lumber to build a road of wood across America.

Mapleton

Every year, the mayor runs a contest
to see who can guess the annual rainfall.
After a few good storms, the Siuslaw rises
drowning Helen McCready's prize tulips.
The rowboat tied to her front porch
is again useful. She has no intention of moving.
Helen was born in this house, and so was her mother.
Her patience is stronger than the current.
From the back porch, she fishes for salmon.

Neskowin

Gulls hang against the wind, shift
and are gone.

A thin wave, a dazzling curtain,
turns the white shore brown.

I continue building the castle.
The moat has filled with water.
Under siege, outer walls crumble.
The highest tower flies a blue feather!

Tired of defeat, I retreat up the beach
to climb on driftwood large as whalebones.

I turn a stump upside down: roots,
a kind of sculpture—the trunk
stretching deep
so branches may reach
far into the earth.

Nehalem

Along the bay, snags,
gray totems, still stand
where land sunk
during the last great quake
three centuries ago.

Saltwater rushed in
drowning them.
Osprey fish
from these spires.

They endure the rain,
an occasional hurricane,
baking sun,
and like ordinary people,
blend in—
taken for granted.

Rockfishing

Beyond the first row of breakers
a seal cleaves the surface, only the ebony head
visible, scouting like a periscope.

He stares at me, eyes not blinking,
so I hold up this good sized
red snapper—showing off
one fisherman to another.

Having seen enough
and probably knowing
where there's a salmon to be caught,
he submerges as though towed under
by the current.

The ocean is an endless range of swells—
peaceful—the music from the tide playing
against the rocks.

The pole gives a healthy tug
bending sure as a willow
that's just found water.

You can never tell what you've got.
Could be a few rags of kelp,
or a small shark.

I reel in and by Jesus
if it isn't a Dungeness crab,
a little bigger than my hand.

Like a spider at the end of his thread, he dangles
breast stroking the air.

Further out in the channel,
the fish-seeking missile surfaces
with a Chinook in his mouth.
Then he's off again, a torpedo
seeking a target.

Winter Storm

The ocean is a green fury.
Rain falling

for three days
continues like a habit.

My nerves grow feeble
from lack of sun.

On the hill, shore pine
crippled with age.

I hear the wind honing my bones
clean as driftwood.

A black dog runs down the beach
chasing invisible gulls.

Acknowledgments

These poems first appeared in the following publications:

American Land Forum: "The Spar Tree, The High Climber"

Black Bear: "Cone Picking"

Blast Furnace: "Salmonberry Mountain, 1911"

California Quarterly: "Rockfishing"

Cascadia Rising: "March Weather"

Chiron Review: "Ten Feet of Rain"

Colorado-North Review: "Neskowin"

Echoes: "Hanging Up the Spurs, the Tree Topper"

Elohi Gadugi: "Mapleton"

Forbidden Peak: "Rain Country," "Tillamook Burn, 1933"

FutureCycle: "Celilo Falls"

Greenfield Review: "Logging the Umpqua, the Tree Topper"

Half Drunk Muse: "The Daily Forecast,"

Lunarosity: "Escape"

Pedestal Magazine: "David Hill Road"

Perigee: "Dawson Pond"

Poets On-line: "Widow-makers"

South Florida Poetry Review: "Marcola Ridge"

Trajectory: "Late July, Harvest"

Trillium: "Finley's Pasture"

Turtle Island Quarterly: "Logging Camp: 1921"

Umbrella: "Hiking the Wilson River Trail"

Untitled Country: "Wilson River: First Outing after Quadruple Bypass"

Walt's Corner: The Long Islander: "Nehalem," "Thatcher Road"

Windfall: "Arlington, Oregon, 1956," "Columbus Day Storm," "Elegy for a Common Field"

Woodrose: "Winter Storm"

Writers Dojo: "Eastern Oregon"

Special thanks to Tim Applegate, Lars Nordstrom, Ralph Salisbury, Penelope Scambly Schott, and Ingrid Wendt for their wisdom and support. Also, love to my wife, Carole, for all her help on this artistic journey.

Praise for *Stronger Than the Current*

Mark Thalman sets us working in the wet woods of Oregon. We feel the bark, smell the smoke, hear the saws, and watch as *rain glistens like salmon scales/ on the tip of an eagle's beak.* These vignettes of the 1920s through 60s relive the beauty and passing of a wilder heritage. I was moved and haunted by "Arlington, Oregon, 1956," where a boy imagines the Columbia rising behind John Day Dam, his mother telling him, *everything will be under water/ like the castle in your fishbowl.* And I worried, smiled and cheered for Helen McCready of "Mapleton." Though she loses her prize tulips to the surging Siuslaw, she ties a rowboat to the porch, remains *stronger than the current* and casts for salmon. These well-crafted poems embody the simple, indestructible beauty of Oregon and its people.

—Henry Hughes
Oregon Book Award Winner

These sturdy, brief, plainspoken poems have a distinctive Made-in-Oregon stamp to them. There are logging poems and landscape poems—weather and landscape figure prominently in them—and poems of Oregon history. The "Tillamook Burn" and "Celilo Falls" . . . and "Finley's Pasture" where *Four Belgians, ebony titans, long retired,/ graze the green pasture.* Modest, quiet poems, unassuming, but rich in substance and detail, like a good meal they stick with you.

—Clemens Starck, Oregon Book Award Winner
and author of *Cathedrals & Parking Lots*

About the Author

Mark Thalman is the author of *The Peasant Dance* (Cherry Grove Collections, 2020) and *Catching the Limit* (Fairweather Books, 2009). His work has been widely published for four and a half decades. His poems have appeared in the *Paterson Review*, *The MacGuffin*, *Pedestal Magazine*, and *Valparaiso Review*. He is the editor of poetry.us.com.

Thalman received his MFA in Creative Writing from the University of Oregon, then taught English and Creative Writing in the public schools for 35 years and is now retired. Thalman lives in Forest Grove, Oregon.

<markthalman.com>

About The Poetry Box®

The Poetry Box® is a boutique publishing company in Portland, Oregon, who provides a platform for both established and emerging poets to share their words with the world through beautiful printed books and chapbooks.

Feel free to visit the online bookstore (thePoetryBox.com), where you'll find more titles including:

Broadfork Farm by Tricia Knoll

Many Sparrows by donnarkevic

Like the O in Hope by Jeanne Julian

Bee Dance by Cathy Cain

The Very Rich Hours by Gregory Loselle

Shadow Man by Margaret Chula

Between States of Matter by Sherry Rind

November Quilt by Penelope Scambly Schott

A Long, Wide Stretch of Calm by Melanie Green

Sitting in Powell's Watching Burnside Dissolve in Rain by Doug Stone

The Kingdom of Birds by Joan Colby

and more . . .

www.ingramcontent.com/pod-product-compliance
Lightning Source LLC
LaVergne TN
LVHW012129070526
838202LV00056B/5926